# DAVID & GOLIATH

## 1 Samuel 17 for children

Written by Martha Streufert Jander
Illustrated by Richard Wahl

Arch® Books
Copyright © 1994, 2003 Concordia Publishing House
3558 S. Jefferson Avenue, St. Louis, MO 63118-3968
Manufactured in Colombia

Philistines were the enemies of
God's people long ago.
They planned to kill God's followers;
They were an evil foe.

God's army saw a sight one day
That made them quake with fright;
A giant—nine feet tall—appeared!
He was an awesome sight.

Goliath was the giant's name;
Oh, how he ranted and roared.
And just the armor he wore weighed
A hundred pounds and more.

Goliath shouted, "Come out and fight;
And if I win, you'll see
That you will all become our slaves;
But if you win—you're free!"

God's army shook, they shook with fear;
They turned to run away.
There was no soldier brave enough;
No soldier who would stay.

But then appeared a shepherd boy—
Yes, David was his name.
He was braver than the men;
He put them all to shame.

"Goliath speaks against our God!
How can we let him go?
I'll fight the giant by myself!
I'm not afraid, you know."

King Saul heard what David said,
And told him, "You're too small.
Goliath is a fighting man.
Goliath's much too tall."

But David knew that when he fought,
His God was always near.
Saul offered David armor, but
He dumped it with no fear.

Then to the brook young David went
And chose five round, smooth stones.
Goliath saw him and he bragged,
"Boy, I'll break your ev'ry bone."

"You come at me," young David called,
"With javelin and sword.
I come at you now in the name
Of the almighty Lord.
It's God who saves and God who gives—
The battle is the Lord's!"

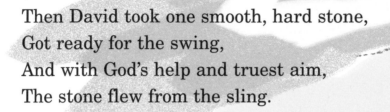

Then David took one smooth, hard stone,
Got ready for the swing,
And with God's help and truest aim,
The stone flew from the sling.

It hit Goliath, square and true.
He fell with a loud cry.
Both armies saw the Lord in charge;
They saw the giant die.

The Philistines then turned and ran—
There was no place to hide.
God's army won the victory,
For God was on their side.

No more giant in the land.
No army they could see.
No enemy that took a stand.
God set His people free!

DEAR PARENTS:

Children enjoy the story of David and Goliath as an adventure story. At first reading, they might easily identify with David as the "super hero." Explain to your children that David was confident, not in his own ability, but in the power of God, who had always protected him and helped him win his battles.

Your children might have some giant fears of their own. David himself said, "When I am afraid, I will trust in You" (Psalm 56:3). Encourage your children to share their fears openly. Then pray together, secure in the knowledge that God provides for all your needs.

Jesus conquered tremendous giants for us, giants powerful enough to rob us of life with Him. Through His crucifixion and resurrection, Jesus conquered sin, death, and the power of the devil. Rejoice with your children as you celebrate our victory—the victory we have already won in Jesus.

THE EDITOR